The Sudden Quiet

Also by Fraser Mackay
Opus at 4
New Skin
The Kelly Show (One Act Play)
Made it This Far
Going Home

Fraser Mackay
The Sudden Quiet
Selected Poems

Acknowledgements

To Rhonda Baum for her keen artist's eye.
To Barry Hill and Robert Drummond for asking the hard questions.
To Kate Butler for her generous critiques.
To Lee Beckworth and Chris Lawrance for their friendship
and writerly support.

The Sudden Quiet: Selected Poems
ISBN 978 1 76041 932 5
Copyright © text Fraser McKay 2020
Cover art: Rhonda Baum

First published 2020 by
Ginninderra Press
PO Box 3461 Port Adelaide 5015 Australia
www.ginninderrapress.com.au

Contents

From *New Skin*

Thursday scattered rain	11
grit	12
you know my name	13
jacket	14
skirting the penumbra	15
minestrone	16
Indian grocery store Monday night	17
song of future whales	18
lone angel	19
you want	20
candlelight	21
Sunday again & the cricket	22
Monday at the well	23
7 seconds to logic	25
within reach	26
black swan	27
pondering 42	28
12:58 a.m.	30
hinterland	31
intruder	32
the listening hills	33
inheritance	34
gliding to town	35
Tuesday after the war	36
turned off lately	37
night tennis	38
blue sky vein	39
crucifixion	40
snaking home	41

swinging always	42
food – buildings	43
marking the lambs	44
western forecast	45

From *Opus at 4*

song of wire	49
new rock	50
solidarity	51
opus at 4	52
landscape	53
a notion of eternity	55
not bin a horse round 'ere in years	56
equanimity	57
in apron and wires	58
Semaphore Beach	59
conversations with Bert	60
leaving	61
dead tree	62
the sudden quiet	63
mortise	64
night	65
dance me out of here	66
horses	67
crane	69
cumulus gather like bullies	70
choughs	71
the ocean doesn't need us	72
arriving	73
business	74
homeless	75
driving away	76

along the contour	77
art or death	78

From *Made It This Far* and *Going Home*

as is	81
twilight	84
resolve	85
cherry plum time	86
going home	87
the swallow	88
weird uncle	89

From *New Skin*

Thursday scattered rain

lately rather slow off the blocks
labouring against the dyslexic tide
I turn on careful feet
so as to not disturb the frost
then unannounced
cockies in the treetops
break into a racket of screeching
then stop just as suddenly.

grit

the stars are out tonight Rachael
and I'm moving again, away from life
Latin-stepping the moonlit quartz

this bleak equation, distanced
from ownership, hunted, wearied
falling heavily in the shadows

formlessness, isn't it?
this striving, pieces breaking off
but with a sense of standing firm
the letting go woven into the fabric.

you know my name

some want what art is
perhaps love
question what qua qua is
to shed cloak of indifference
of small bearded knowing
the pact in delirium made

want beauty
is what they seek
attempt
mask fear
to turn on thoughts
the casket lowered

Al's sailor's grin said – *it happened once it could
happen again* – adding as I descended the stairs
and it's nigh on Easter – but there was no resurrection
and the ghost ship   in search of an ocean
lumbered on   through the treacherous   evening news

jacket

listening at all angles
this aching loss of intimacy
traumas subtext

holds me in check
the coo coo of little doves
leaks into the afternoon

later the phone
exploded on the slate
the shift nurse arrived

sorry to disturb ya, luv, she said
it's all right, I'm often disturbed
that jacket not too tight? no, it's fine.

skirting the penumbra

the prickly spring sun
dips below the veranda
Julie moves with her books and water
to the shade in the corner

our words quietly skirt
the penumbra of our lives
float out to the cherry orchard
brush past the ancient trunks

those wearied disciples
the scant sap barely enough
to relieve their burden of limbs
– bronze-wings at the dam

the evening turns pink and red
fat cloud galleons lumber in
fill the horizon, their fiery sails
ignite the western sky.

minestrone

feeling the weight
a tin of beans
in my hand
wondered how you're doing
I saw Tom at the Dhol concert
he asked if you'd moved in
I told him you're staying in the Gong
a small wave of melancholy
washed over
the banks of my equilibrium

this week lighter
days alone
making minestrone
I miss our intimacy
autumn is here
long walks
scattered leaves
content with small movements

perhaps another evening
whist preparing a meal
it will come to me…
ah yes – so that's what it was all about
then get on with peeling vegetables.

Indian grocery store Monday night

Indian grocery store Monday night
long weekend traffic crawls through
this postcard town – shelves stacked
with neatly packaged slices of non-reality

across the screen flash unbroken hearts
full of artful bliss – stumbling today
like a camel with four left feet
trying to approach my mind, to re-hinge
this broken gate – later to unravel my emotions
father and son, the sense and the nonsense

a sunny day, the front yard, curled foetus like
on the ground against the grey paling fence
the ethereal beauty of fragrant roses
washed over the afternoon – the first boot
thudded in, breaking the slow silence

with every slight movement the universe pulsates
Indian grocery store Monday night
good angle on Lydiard – between appointments
in the dusk a solitary neon blazes
I'm eating a samosa at the laminex
the attendant behind the counter
his head craned back, watches
Bollywood on the big screen.

song of future whales

sometime before enlightenment
        brain gone, pencil resting
                Monday or Wednesday morning
                        familiar world, loving, but
                        fragmented or another word
                pull it closer, that other life
        name it…grace…a presence
the indifferent landscape

and finding yourself
as detached as the landscape
a respite from the day's
grim-faced radio news

resting from the inner game
        in remembrance of a love buried deep
                in the ocean, your soul and sustenance
                      for generations of future whales
                      but meanwhile a fragile hand
                moves about the cluttered sink
        a voice singing from afar
perhaps a whale song.

lone angel

when I lose myself, I find myself
the words broken, the sentences in disarray
ideas, images smudged like thoughts
dissolved in their own ether, black smears
black like night, bereft of stars, but that's not right
there are always stars – stars and angels

gulls cry out at sea, wheel on the wind
the lost boys unseen bump into deck chairs
stumble over sunbathers, push out
from the centre, struggle to free themselves
they spill onto the late afternoon bitumen
homeless, aimless, to stagger arm in arm
trapped in their formlessness
along the gun barrel highway

a seagull hovers, detached and clear
turns and glides to the bluff

today, talking in the wilderness – talking quietly
so as not to disturb the universe
I have a song in my heart and when I sing it
will the stars fall into place?

I met her at the funeral of a friend
the electricity of coincidence
begs closer attention – we lay
mesmerised by death's lustre
in the diffused light of that cheap hotel

honour has it own reward – but still
this dull ache climbs in and out of my heart.

you want

you want everyday
                               your language on my tongue
you want more
              than I can pay
                               your tongue in my ear
       the wild blue sea

christ wouldn't you love
                          to feel god-like?
your future death hangs
                         dragging from dawn to dusk
anger's old carcass
                         up and down my street
all you want
       beyond this world
                             are you
receiving my friend
                  the universe
my tongue in your ear
                       the wild blue sea?

candlelight

in mauve shadows of evening
reading Ondaatje by candlelight
this scared little ant with a sore thumb

words of affection scribbled beneath
yellow painted suns
a gift from my grandchildren.

Sunday again & the cricket

the artist has moved camp
another tender twig, broken
left for a rescued two/thirds

this morning Uncle Carl called from St Petersburg
he'd just been to the opera – on the way back to the hotel
he was robbed by Russian louts and earned a split lip

Sunday again and the cricket
happily drowned in the mother-lode
quietly indoors, phone unplugged
blue sky solitude, stretching
to the edge of the world – 3 for 81
oh joy, awash in the plenitude
happy happy happy

two grabbed and held him whilst two accomplices
emptied his pockets, he lost all perspective and he lost
his voice when he tried to call out to his companions
who were ascending on an escalator to the next level

Sunday again and the cricket
wind comes in sharp percussive gusts
the dog's asleep in its box
drops of red jewels in a wire frame
tap against the terracotta's curve – 3 for 126

when the robbers let him go he headed off
to catch up with his friends to share his adventure
on turning around the robbers it seemed
had dematerialised into the dark and ominous
Russian night – but he is well, although
a little shaken – and sends his love.

Monday at the well

1

august tail of winter lashes the farm
fills the silence between the blades
but among the honey scented jonquils
there is a detached, calmness of mind
like the graffiti said…*to dance*

2

early robin on wattle branch
forest cries of yellowtails
the curved backs of two grey 'roos
their mouths work the themeda
pull themselves forward with tender hands

3

in the vineyard clipping the wily growth
cuts ooze sap, over Ben Nevis
a storm looms, thoughts scud east
familiar circles, reasons not so hard

to pry loose, dash for shelter
for the sacred poetry at your elbow
the last straggler trimmed and wired
as the first drops slap the iron

4

feet up, immersed in words – bliss hangs
on the constant hook – a reference leads
to Wright – hungrily turn pages
to revisit Eliot, distracted by Scott…

horses heavy hooves now stamp outside
then an impatient snort, they've come for carrots
a daily visit; I stroke Kate's powerful neck
pat her soft mouth – *what big teeth you have*
crunch and dribble – *these carrots are organic*
I hope you appreciate that
a quiet day, in a particularly uneventful year
scant gigs, taxation zero, not even a parking fine
the evening meal bubbles on the stove
I reach for my guitar, a mouse
pokes its head out from behind the cupboard
and looks up as if to say –

ah, just the two of us again?

7 seconds to logic

in my peripheral vision
> a blur that was my father
> descended from the cereal box
> and crumpled into the linoleum floor

in the hallway, uniformed trees bustled
> arms and eyebrows danced with concern
> a tunnel of fire rose in my throat
> along Kilgour Street the ambulance
> wailed childhood's last refrain

I didn't often visit the ward in which
> my mother would end her days
> but one afternoon as we watched
> the fattest of storm clouds
> drift across the Northcote sky

she turned and smiled and the words
> *going home soon*
> fell strangely from her lips.

within reach

for Jo

remember the brown snake we discovered
in the extension? I was impressed

by your curiosity, enjoying the spectacle
one metre of writhing muscular beauty

when it slid beneath a cupboard
I gingerly stepped into the unfinished room
and opened the outer door, to facilitate its escape

then we walked 40 minutes along bush tracks
to Antonio's, for coffee and cake

on returning I climbed into my CFA overalls
and armed with a good stick made a thorough search
but the reptile seemed to have departed

your drum Jo
your beat, yesterday's tears on your shoulder
darkness flaps her great cloak, time apart
our time together, unexpected gifts it all adds up

but hey I'm tired of numbers
let them pass nameless disappearing

I just want to
        hear your voice like
                      the morning bell
chiming the hour
            descending
                    the singing stairs.

black swan

for LB

1

summer rain sizzles the tarmac
another coffee? – your grey-eyed love
curls around my loss, finish this letter
then drive home – *go home*, you said
grinning through a blond lock

an empty boat bobs at the mooring
caffeine weary – a fat tome on the balmy couch
slip into the depths, barely a glance

2

foam hissed along the bluff
an unquenchable ragged line
the harsh chastening light
I bent to dabble the brine

turned my back to the endless sea
a hidden rock bloodied my knee
I struggle to leave you behind

3

morning, I walk the glen road
the dull ache of a familiar wound
knowing too well, the feel of your shadow
the texture of your absence.

pondering 42

dear Larry…hope all is well in Mullumbimby
(I'll just shut the window, damn noisy out there)
did I spell that right, my Greek isn't too flash
well as predicted, last week our team
was rather disassembled by a bunch
of fine young players
but it certainly improved my game

then the other night investigating
another sighting up in the hills
late, near Van Every's ruins
but nothing doing when I got there
just the usual darkness you know
and the stars winking – so I winked back
anyway on my return negotiating a steep incline
my phone rang and at the same time
I heard what I thought could only be
the much feared
                    Blaspheming
                              Beaufort
                                    Bunyip

as I turned to greet my fate
I slipped on a patch of damp moss
twisting badly my ankle and after expiring a little
French, I crawled painfully down the hill
up the stairs and into bed
needless to say I woke many times
during the night pondering 42

but further my sleep was broken
fielding phone calls from the disconsolate one
floating on waves of melancholic reason
breaking down and redefining her self
and her pain whereupon I asked in my most
caring vocal – exactly where does it hurt?
but it's closed anyway – you know – the door
yet still her energy surges despite the ledger's
disapproval – so here I wait waiting, amidst
beauty's fleeting images, sans emotional projections
keeping myself tidy, but alas still no letter
from you – was it something I said?

– love as always, to you and your intimates.

12:58 a.m.

12:58 a.m., lee kwo wrote, *and what if this life is death – will I have the courage to love this death as much as I have loved this life?*

so sooner rather than later hey uncle?
time is a funny thing – like cash
never enough, never too much
compassionate speaking dada Buddha

dada shoulda coulda given some good news
where were you biff boy, all these years dying?

12.58 a.m. detached from the torso
from the tree, detached from belief
leaving undisturbed the dust
                                on the windowsill.

hinterland

cicadas hang in the mistletoe tree
lifeless kin list on the empty tide

dusted with lime, the stench of equus
rises from a roadside ditch – struggling
against the constellations – I've lost
my centre – my four-stringed woman

at the billabong, hard bliss behind my eyes
cockatoos gather in the threads
of my brave assertions, shredding them
with the glee of recalcitrant children

back home, horses mill about
Hamish lame – a recipient perhaps
of a well aimed hoof – I hammer
the swivel-hinge into the post
rehang the rusted pipe-wire gate
it closes with a satisfying click.

intruder

      the plaited wire on the old gate
      frames waves of wispy drosera
float fairy-like on the morning hill

another day
      another draft
            eat breakfast

it's been a long time
      since I sold my guns
      and slipped unnoticed
into a quiet life

these mountains
      exude a tough beauty
      they suit my oblique nature
if that's what it is

I dreamed last night
      I placated the black mare
      but she wouldn't release
my hand from her mouth.

the listening hills

i.m. Bert Milne

another day, driving out
to straighten up the paddocks
high on the granite – chewing a blade
the red-streaked dawn, nestles a cradle of stars

*if you can't help out your neighbour
what's the point of being here?*

the autumn sun warmed
his crimson leathery neck
his nut brown arm

one late afternoon
when sombre light obscured
aberrant notions of time
he slipped away, like mist
seeping into a compliant paddock.

inheritance

endless stretch of bitumen
bisects hard flat paddocks
an eternity of posts and wire

miles before
a neighbour's bereft eyes
among familiar names
carved in marble slabs

set back from the road
an evening star
the beacon glow
of a solitary Mallee homestead

like their forebears
their blood runs drought, despair
failed crops, a life taken
by quiet hands

about an hour to go
a farmer and his wife
silenced by the precarious distance
gathered between them.

gliding to town

gliding to town
the welcome arch of cypress
canopies the black turf

our flaxen-haired children
are coming home
to shoulder the wheel

wild scented roses
cascade the axle tree
Jack (barely 5 years old)
looks me in the eye, and asks,

are you still learning, grandpa?

Tuesday after the war

apocalyptic pails of rain fell
on the mullock's harsh summit
we took stock in a bombed-out orchard
barrels dripped, we glanced about

the torn and empty fields
they seemed to shatter the notion
of that cherished gift: the hard-forged bond
between humans and the universe

it's not easy to explain distance
these algebraic mountains
or the chemical vibrations
that cause blood to run cold

but it's Tuesday after the war
and for me at least it's over
limping now toward medication
resolute, turning away from life
perfecting the old trick, amnesia.

turned off lately

turned off lately your raucous Babylon radio piercing
black-noise redneck half-truths, having found therein
no historic, poetic or otherwise significant music
lacking I suppose the smiling I've made it
                              celebrity high-profile hip

turned off lately the vibrant, sensory feast
of geographically sustainable performance art
fully catered of course (how else to get the buggers there)
exploring the diversity of orchestral hubcap landscapes

later we were treated to a white ute duet
spinning in a vortex of dust and diesel fumes
– a backdrop of theatrical shadows and shafts
of light, cleverly highlighted falling latex koalas

turned off lately without a cooee of hope, having let go
childhood's broken toys, thirsty in hardship, brawny arm
around her wisp of a frame, somehow the universe still
functions, but who really cares?
                            just pass the biscuit tray, will ya.

night tennis

for Corey

riding the moonlit bald hills
away from stealth, the dazzling lobs
breathless rallies, commentaries
at the net, on the weather
and whether or not
the ball caught the line

forgotten before we hit
the Pyrenees, ice on the shoulder
searching for a tune on the radio.

blue sky vein

old crow circling time, lawyer vines strangle the moon
your laughter is dying and blue sky vein is at a premium
the goodwill store down on main road, has been razed
to the ground but you can keep your alibi, your three penny
raptures to yourself – nobody's asking for an account

move on rock-a-bye soul sweet lullaby babe
the days are getting old and your handsome prince
is still holding your dreams to ransom
yeah she went all the way down, to the algebra toxic waste
glowing in the blue lounge, comatose
beyond the fridge, living like a cartoon character
stuck forever in a twilight supermarket queue

now where the hell is that number, she said, she was tired
of all the homesick sailors in the cold evening back streets
in the shadows of the knackery yard, horses snort and shiver
as darkness falls like a guillotine

meanwhile the long-haired ice cream sleek merry-go-round
sideshow freaks had closed up shop and shuffling
weary steps back to the bridge, landlocked sweet lullaby babe
bereft of sonnets, suddenly stopped flicked back a lock
turned saying, *I don't care what you got boy,* over her shoulder
– already gone, her cool hips swaying, disappearing
into the nuclear orange sunset…

turned and stepped into a new dream…
blue sky vein is at a premium, fell out of time
stepped into a new dream.

crucifixion

for Trevor Woods

1

with his death, life gains clarity
principles of lust for the moment
deferred…not jumping anywhere tonight
no pleached limbs in the shady hollow

this day, cheapened by plastic ordeals
our reverence for breath
never seems to gain
the weeping threshold
I have no desire to attend
yet another crucifixion
– bitter cuts with lasting serrations

2

she didn't like him when he was high
his approximations of reality
climbed beyond her grasp

aching to hear the sound of flight
sliding off the snow-bound freeway
he slammed the hurried exit, spinning arms jerked
along the wire – reaching for that seam of light
crying, *yours, Nellie, is not the only galaxy.*

snaking home

word-shedding the well chronicled
minutiae of addiction, in the usual font
dream hands reach out
but my attentive heart advises
you've been gone now a tidy week

across the doona another moon
drapes its casual arm – tomorrow you'll be here
approximately – avoiding heart-spaces
our life slipping with every relocation
under a black hill the future leans precariously
skyward – plunged deep in arrhythmia

I lurch around this broken mind
another skulking fox night to endure
wide awake imagining your headlights
snaking through the pines.

swinging always

I keep a hold   on my life   quietly
in the wet season   juggling
pianola rolls   unmanageable
eyebrows   alarmed
at the frolic   shuffling
feet first   beneath   the harvest moon
explaining   to the ether
the shrieking blades   the bonfire crowd

I keep a hold   on my life
along the forest road   swinging always
                        to the back beat.

food – buildings

the swallows have taken up residence
in their mud nest on the veranda wall
one sits on the eggs, while its mate fetches insects
for lunch, soon we'll be watching you and I
the young ones, their first tentative flutter of wings

lately I've been in excellent spirits and anything
seems possible – even the completion of the bathroom
but give me a break it's only been 4 years and if nothing
else it's a barometer for patience and perhaps engenders
a forgiving nature in my friends

I'm reminded of what this carpenter said at the local pub one
evening when asked by a prospective employer a local farmer
                    – what kind of worker are you?

well I'm slow – said the carpenter – *but I'm rough!*
the farmer's laughter split the bar
he got the job bloody – said Antonio incredulously
that summer, to every fresh set of ears.

marking the lambs

marking lambs
    don't bother me
        bodies sectioned
        hunting throats
        while young smirking boys
        loiter the bank
    their infant testicles
suited up for the carving

dross falls into the burning sky, I watch
        until the dread becomes
        painfully too funny

        beyond this clay
        life dissolves
    and I wonder distractedly
            if we'll leave a stain.

western forecast

Saturday – Cloudy. Winds south to south-westerly. Temperatures during the day around 14 degrees Celsius.

I woke early – a sense of impending euphoria
having completed my last psychology unit
now back to colours, framing the universe

I have a friend who inspires me to delve deeper
into my core, walk in the mountains – or just be still

watch the mob of grey 'roos – back-dropped against
the lush green slope, 4 mothers – joeys in pouches
a few juveniles and a big papa – fur-lined muscular
curves – grazing, unselfconsciously alert

red Larrys haggle at the feeder – scatter when
I wander out to fetch wood – the 'roos clear off too
later I work a chapter, pull a few weeds – your red
shoes catch my eye – I bring them inside

*Isolated showers contracting to the coast this evening.
There are no current warnings.*

From *Opus at 4*

song of wire

for V

the indecision of blue clouds
hangs in winter trees
we wait for rain that never falls

lately death's dulcet tones
have been bothering my good ear
its song of wire, too tired to rust

the sun reaches across
the ochre clay of mid morn
life has yet to show us everything

we edge toward divinity
and why the hell not?
I love our domesticity

the way you pluck the bass
your inward smile
I never know where you are

today old metal dissolves
I wait, alert, detached, case in-hand
carriages rush past, the storm abates
a woman blushes at the news-stand

projecting to journey's end
I see myself latch the gate
and to the shack gain the silent hill.

new rock

I want a new rock
        endowed with
                generous facets
                        and a mind
                        not easily
                        moved
                by knowledge
              and the weight
                of its own
              importance

        I want
your glass ideals
    to shatter
in disbelief
across this
broken
avenue
of our
dead
future.

solidarity

war wrecks pass in the hieroglyphic dawn
listing toward sobriety – unable
to abide, who I thought we were

stifled laughter in the parking lot
eye to eye in the compressed silence
– temper this dumb anger

Fletch at the wheel, tired-drunk, failed
to make the bend, his old wagon slid
sideways down the gully, grazed
a stringy-bark, a rocky outcrop gutted
the sump – found solidarity in a massive
yellow-box gum – black liquid
oozed down the grassy slope

today I tilt at clockwork gnomes
traffic sluggish around the quay
can't complain I'm too busy – wasting
precious breath, ruminating on death.

opus at 4

nothing like expected the universe
glimpsed from side-on waiting
for some ephemera to clutch
hosanna like run a giddy mile

ice formed in these unexpected hours
a vision of Scott dead at the pole
his dog tied to a sled huddled against
a bitter death

on the mainland night shadows
slid the tarmac white doves
circled the black-slashed-dross-fallen-sky

this madness is not authentic
yesterday's grey wash go outside
pull a few weeds forget
about yourself for a while

landscape

words – shaped   time-framed
traverse deeper   into calm
communicate   choice – intent

consider the recluse who occupies
space – speculates   in words
his solitude   the landscape

a farmer doesn't 'try' and plough the lower forty
fit – devise – articulate   your understanding
of silence – the leaf, the stone, the blade of grass

the shack now comes into view, the window
the tree and that awkward space between

we ponder linguistically the aesthetic experience
the alignment of decisions real or imagined
the connection of gender (a man thinks about
                         a woman for instance)

we should've planted vegetables – but October's
already in the door, anyway the locusts are coming
– is that what you'd call an existential event?

no I'm not suggesting that locusts
are existentialists and can you pick up
some carrots from the store – please?

at the window – his insignificance framed
the carpenter considers, that without a jamb
the possibility   of a door
is structurally   problematic

and without a window, the vista remains
unframed – but we are afforded
a less encumbered view of ourselves
the wind visibly colludes – rushes about
parting grasses, rustling leaves – unsettles
the horses and some humans – unable to say

feelings – overwhelmed by landscape, thought
– adjuncts that distract the meandering eye
the heady fragrance of brewed coffee

naked, she turns at the window – shall we go?
he notes: the elements of distance, an atomic illusion
the earth confined within its sphere of blue.

a notion of eternity

firm in stirrup along the ridge
weave through slender white trunks
a hawk lifts from a fence post
gracefully lopes to the treeline

winter has come to the mountains
a fire blazes for his children–
candlelit notions – self-respect

down the track, leather creaks
– words pile up snow-deep
mouths move without forks
without appetite – at the summit
the ranges unfold – reveal distance
with no purpose underfoot
he rides the long way home

everything but the truth!
quiet knives menace the dark
a cold wind cuts like a cure
grieving a life he couldn't save.

not bin a horse round 'ere in years

the difficult science of a troubled son
two brothers, two bodies
                autumn wind bends
                the drought-dry grass

dingoes snap and snarl
the void is palpable
                police cars in the drive, suggest
                that reality curves away

they say it probably won't rain till spring
                we abandon the dead
                and eventually, our memories
after the hearing they lead him
back to the cell – the story
                commands a scant note
                we are reminded – that the press
                feeds only on fresh corpses

the evening sun drops into a dry dam
a spider dangles on a thread.

equanimity

winter sun slides through the bi-fold doors
below the blade – the salve stings his back
the sun creeps now over Pownceby's
old kitchen table – passes through

the crockery cabinet's glass door
the bush nurse arrives to change his dressing
he makes coffee, they share news
white plates glow like flying-saucers
cut glass reflects flints of light – sharp
v's tattoo the side of the cast-iron stove
from the steps he watches her negotiate

the creek crossing, then he ambles hill-ward
to read in the late morning sun
'the back country' tucked under his arm.

in apron and wires

dock weed twists on the dull breeze
an easterly swirls the foothills
collides head-on into a northerly
aberrant maps menace my brow

sharp light cracks a familiar ocean
hunger softens yesterday's grief
but I'm falling ahead of myself – I forgot
to breathe your name on the podium
a vampire bat descends into my sleep
settles weightless in my hand
its tiny claw wraps around my finger

tonight I muscle through stars
rearrange the cuckoo darkness
and tomorrow in apron and wires

I'll cut you out of my windswept
notions – cut you out of the old
skin box – where I no longer fit.

Semaphore Beach

after the Turner show – ice cream
cones – Semaphore Beach
a dark roiling cloud moved down
St Vincent's Gulf – veils of rain fell
out at sea – white caps pushed
a small craft in their wake

between water and sky – a salty light
– he imagined dancing in the sand
with his lover – around the matted clumps
of seaweed – one big as a car

Turner might be perplexed – to see
his name splashed across elevator doors
on the sides of buses – but he
would've raved in the ethereal light

his mistress – a plain woman we're told
cooked a sustaining porridge, then he'd
wander abroad, with paints and brushes
his belly afire, to inhabit the landscape

Anton's back porch Saturday evening
a broken sky brings the rain inland
the consensus being – we preferred
his later works, their gesture of light
on a low table – the exhibition catalogue
three creased tickets, an empty water bottle.

conversations with Bert

I arrive at the gate – the horses
canter across the creek flat – grass-yellow
paddocks sprawl to the mountain

of the autumn break Bert said, *if we don't
get rain by the Warrnambool Races –
first week in May – then we won't until June*

and of a local wastrel – and not without
compassion he said, *I dunno,
if he was a horse you'd shoot him…*

sunflower seeds tinkle on the metal tray
a buried reptilian insect
writhes up through the spaces

dry autumn days drift listlessly
into winter – no feed to speak of
the horses hang about the shack
snorting – pawing at the dusty ground.

leaving

her heart in retreat, she sleeps now, beneath
a river of blood, detached from appetite
from the bonds of becoming – the earth
holds fast in its trajectory – across the face of art

the horses went mad when she left
their frenzied tails flicked the sky

– for their children he became the waiting
concrete ideals raged against winter longing
if he'd been a swimmer – he would've ridden
the waves – but life's rhythm – too often elusive

in the yard, the dog stirs, rises, languidly stretches
– from the balcony he projects into the landscape
glides lengthwise the undulations – white wings
curve in flight, cut through the early light.

dead tree

22 July

he cuts a Humboldt notch, then back-cuts
through the trunk, the tree stands interminably
a statue with time – then he leaps, the chainsaw
tumbles, a cat-o'-nine-tails branch stings his neck

he picks up the saw – starts it with one rip
cuts rounds – self-possessed
welts smarting – their son looks on

in the evening he walks the hill's scalp
alone, a sense of peace
happy to coexist with the unknowable.

the sudden quiet

hours curve away – thoughts curl up fetal-like
behind a stack of old newspapers – through window grime
the river is ablaze – a spooked mare stamps and whinnies

street music fills the room, you watch the moon
entranced by shape and shadow, you attempt to think
but you feel heavy in space, you crave a story with grit

a child watches his grandfather work the jackknife
he'd bought it as a lad – *you could shave with it*, he sometimes said

he slices an apple, hands the quarters to his grandchildren
you and Celeste – sweet firm apples from his orchard
he looks directly at Celeste, she says *thank you, grandpa*
he frowns as he remembers a time where he cut
                              deeper than necessary

3 p.m. a tourist rises to leave, her scarf catches
on the chair, mandarins spill from the bench – you are
running smooth – the medication – so far so good
there's a bunch of tables to clear and you know
two candles won't last the night

then like steady rain your emotions – a blood-rush
to the kitchen, to build an apricot house – a witch's hat roof
juxtaposed with last night's dream – random images
break through – contextualise the silence – a deserted
playground, the grey veranda boards, his empty chair.

mortise

by the last bed he'll ever sleep in
she sits, holding his gaze – gnarled hands
clutch at breath – he asks after Vlad's dog
music seeps in…he hums, nods…
– *no more dancing,* he grins

                    dawn on the veranda
                    drops fall from the mouth
                    of a kangaroo drinking at the dam

inside on the window ledge
a timber mortise – the shadowed plane
faces into the room – she traces
the wood's texture – the slot
fashioned by hand drill and chisel
held by fingers she can no longer touch.

night

sheltered from life's critical eye
I lay inside your shadow – cool air sighs
through the bedroom window
quartz gleams on the ridge
one day we'll become the contours
of a south-easterly breeze, until then

– the contrived pain of being
but tonight I feel fine – I pull you in close
kiss your sleeping shoulder, loving you
– your doubts, your courage – watch
a moon shadow traverse the hill.

dance me out of here

JFK's last ride, live
on the radio – mother
was 'away' – the old man
made porridge, it was
too salty, other things
cut-in, real or imagined
it was briefly
              1963

drove west in '79, hooked
on literature and self-belief
Glass turned up his amplifier
we posted rambling letters
              back east

the moon was up for it
a satellite dish full of Warhol
and where Miller once loomed
Bukowski now muscled the
              landscape

lovers hung on against hope
and good sense, rousing times
drunk on late night Olivettis
our lips burned, to celebrate
              to forget.

horses

And the hood of the horses shakes the crumbling field as they run –
Virgil

I never forget being born, the B-52's lumbering approach
carbon-arc lights glared deep into my mother's womb
hurriedly wrapped in a prickly grey blanket – in turns
bumped, jostled and squeezed – we taxied to the hangar
the great metal door swung open with a sharp crack
 the balmy night air of a new life

I never forget with my brother Eddie, riding the horses
of our youth, at one with the power of the sun
a kinship, kept at reins' length

I never forget the day Eddie left home – blood streamed
down the old man's face – cursing Eddie all the way to the
end of our street – next thing I was riding inside a fat creaky
whale bussing down the east coast – the hot summer wind
leaked in through the cracks – the thoughts in my head did
their creepy gymnastics – three days later finished the pills
and spilled onto the tarmac at Central Station

I'm amazed now at what pages I landed on – life was enemy
drones coming over the hill – scars appeared without
reference, renegade emotions, jerky staccato behaviours
I got older, I had willing ears, I made friends down one-way
streets, I picked up the pen and found beauty in the world
then one day in the Alexandra Gardens I met Rachel

I never forget weekends by the river – the sun glanced off her dazzling white skin, her limbs were strong and lithe – she had a yen for jazz and country walks – we went dancing every Friday night – I allowed her to move fractionally closer

Rachel loved to sit on the bar of my bike – my arms around her as I steered the machine through the meat and three veg evening streets – I thought we were going to the stars – but then one foggy 3 a.m. the Dance Club was razed to the ground – sirens wailed, rushing uniforms and writhing hoses filled the road – it was the day before St Valentine's

like a mauling from a mass of priests I never forget the gaggle of thesis waving shrinks splitting hairs over which box to shove me in – as it turned out I was leaping with my own tricks, usually in the afternoon, seeking clarity in thoughtless concentration, standing on one leg looking due east, in the pose of a pointer

I never forget the grief in Rachel's eye, years later on the Corso, where a chance meeting stopped us in mid-flight – we just stared at each other until wordlessly she turned and fled – I never forget riding in the mountains, the horses of my youth – a freedom, like forgiveness.

crane

for RB

cockatoos attend the sky
we move down the ridge
your words evoke light

a crane's feather, afloat on the dam
just out of reach – the wind is in
the south-west – in time it'll drift to the bank

– we went back later, your touch
hovered like euphoria, the horses
moved in and out of tree shadows
the feather bobbed at the bank –
another lay in the grass nearby.

cumulus gather like bullies

to strike up a conversation with would-be suicides, Angel Don of the Gap would ask, 'can I help you in some way?'

engine-drift high over desert plains, tarmac slaps the planet
he's done the binary, cold code exponential – spin's the factor
big swoop on the long table…

back in the tomb he works an esoteric equation, repeats
the knot, heartbeat falters, cool coke-eye watches dives
talks to his teeth, predicts a barrow full down to the night vault
emotions calibrated, edges back from colour's spinning luck

waits for the late bus, living for nothing – path forward
sleety sleepless September southbound #19 – glazed eyes swim
in proximity – premeditated star jump to breach death's void
broken fatigued boyo disbelief, shallow of breath – confined by
four white walls – a child dreams – his brother's tough love
low voices, the squeak of disinfected floors, an odour he loathes
ascends from coma, still inhabiting the old skin

to learn again death's an unreliable ally, old words resonate
in his bones, assault his thoughts, tease him with a collage
of logic so abstract his head throbs – trouble's arrived no going back

grey-black cumulus gather like bullies, jostle each-other snarling
taunts, a vile bunch – just get in, do the job, then get the hell out
thought cauterised longing switches off, hits dead space, black-wall
despair – kicks in horrific disbelief, fingers curled in the rope.

choughs

nobody in the lane –
above the treetops
a cockatoo banks a slow arc

wood choughs float on the air – in ethereal
black cloaks they alight on the dry grass
– a gathering of plaintive cries

my friend arrives, frayed – spiked
laughter's desolation rattles the glass
incrementally I become present

tomorrow resides on a dusty shelf
hungry for succour, I wander – a fallen leaf
a dark crevice among the stones

* The white-winged wood chough is a large, almost completely black bird. It has a curved beak, a red eye and a large white wing-patch, which is seen when the bird is in flight. They occur throughout eastern and south-eastern mainland Australia.

the ocean doesn't need us

slow walk back from c-space – mixed bag humans
late on the web, dodging strange portals – in real life
a tidy arrangement, maybe best we can expect

dust plumes hang in shafts of evening light
locate truth, arrive at conclusion, extrapolate
course of action, go to bed – morning swirl of grain

for the clucky one – season turning – embers
smoulder deep in heart's fragile landscape
begin small, stretch a finger, a slow kata
I miss our camaraderie – two sharp rocks
we couldn't live together, tremors sent us reeling
– night flexing on Barkly, probing tender connections

house red, bruschetta, traffic detours
a young cop, face at ground level, her eyes
look into mine; *can you get up?*

arriving

I make a pile of black-wattle bark – collect
kindling – stack wood – morning solitude
counters the weight of uncertainty

a magpie pecks at the turf – runs staccato
down the spring-green slope – thoughts
stagger about, I parry contrived burdens

tender of heart, an hour fills with years
a labyrinth of unknowable lives
shadows move about the treeline
curious face to the world, I hold a question
light plays the page's crease – no answer
for the life between my ribs – the challenge of kin

the proximity of ghosts – in tones of gratitude
I cross the dawn-lit field – I have become a lonely river
perhaps I should have planned for this eventuality
                – embrace the life that abandons.

business

artless days go by
your moon-book jaw
cuts through cold space

        lured to the suburbs
        like peasants closed with belief
        we go about unremarkable business

                moonlight slides down weatherboards
                clouds scud across the frosted yard
                the 8.20 rumbles past the kitchen window

                        in the late-night supermarket
                        Ekke said, *you need a list?*
                        I shrug – it's just me, you know.

homeless

the old man cleaves into morning's minutiae
an armful of boxwood before breakfast
he squints to the troubled sky – rivers bleed
life without a face – he recalls the lonely stretch of road
an aged station wagon – windows up tight
butane heater – a pair bound by love
addiction – their dog, the killing frost

                              – disembodied images
drift up from the well – water's memory
gathers our stanzas – its song of rust
hums in the wires – too old for the bridge
for wine – his judgement in arrears, a cracking
sheet of wind hurls through the treetops
the oncoming deluge – hastens him indoors.

driving away

in childhood's small grave
lost to the world – deep
in another page – father too
kept disappearing – but
like a magician, he'd reappear
and from the ether, produce a fist
the discolouration to my teacher
was hard to explain – maybe I
didn't believe it myself – such
a gentle-man – loath to disappoint

>memories flash of running – broken days
>and Rachel – her careless smile
>her beautiful hands on the wheel

tonight stars drink the lake
folded arms guard the tree-house
driven by water, you dream
with a raven – the rampant darkness
has become a bleak truth

an old guy in a dark suit sits mute
beside your sleeping warmth
attentive to longing's dumb pulse
we navigate inadequate language
– the architecture of loss

annoying as it is – we talk about
dead matches left in the box
freight carriages rumble the yard
on the dresser, a glass vial
taps twice against the mirror.

along the contour

they walk euphoric miles, for coffee, knee deep
in sand dunes, the ocean does its lunar thing
radio quiet, without appetite, their conversation
weaves, tangles, a change of light illuminates
a delicate shift in their bond

sizing up the shed's frame, a magpie glides down
lands on the ridge, raised and fixed about a week ago
this summer, 2 snakes, a bushfire, January floods
most days, they read in veranda chairs, swim in the dam

she opens the letter, a beginning of sorts, could easily
fall away, a vacant chair, knife poised, she considers
emotional detachment, a device – her friend said,
a kind of letting go, the trick's in the subtle curve
of the lips, she imagines a kite, the string held just so…

later she follows the contour of a kangaroo trail
by a rocky outcrop, old metal – eroded
black-pitted, she stops to repair the fence
her gypsy hair tied back, boundaries for the heart
on the slope ahead, 2 young 'roos bound away.

art or death

for RD

players chat on the sidelines – I note
the shifting margins of silence – my heart
has its lost shape – a piercing eye drills an ace

dawn creeps in behind curtains
pushes along the whitewashed
mudbrick wall – I rise, light the fire
breakfast alone, empty headed
stretch tennis-tight muscles, water
the garden, pack my bag
Whitlam's gone – his countenance
fills the departure lounge screen
Thursday afternoon airbus throbs
with humanity – wings shadow Uluru
cloud-stories drift by the window
I settle into headphone music
relinquish ownership of world problems.

From *Made It This Far* and *Going Home*

as is

Saturday night, tennis weary, beneath the floorboards, change more than spring in the air, more than hope and dreamy flight, wilderness pressing against the window, no time to ponder the ends the beginnings – royalty cheque cashed and spent in a thrice and yesterday the pump fucked up – I dare not, in any direction, move too fast – the days pile up like broken sentences, life flicks before my eyes, robbed blind, death vaguely understood, time and space held together by fear torn apart by anger, to explain why people die

god knows well the street of first sorrow, laughter and mischief wrested from suffering long toothed coot, bane of child's mirth, hobnailed boots, whip in hand that gloved the fist, the war that never stopped – shadow swooping magpie drawing blood, paperboy entangled with bicycle on the grass, he longed to share but was met with that slap in the face, indifference – nothing sacred here, story's for the telling over the shoulder and to hell with it, we were pushed, punched, jumped and ran scattered to the coast, the city to dwell, lick wounds build dreams to find that life is – and nothing more

this eternity, thinking, scratching, the same itch, lucky to eat to greet, the sunrise without finding truth, without going on – quite simply you said, if you are not free then you are imprisoned – and in our confinement we play no small part

mother died yesterday I felt disconnected conversations with family difficult, reaching out, the gulf so wide, wanting, embracing for an instant then withdrawing, exchanging words picked up along the way, dropped like coins into a poker machine, pull the handle, shrug and walk away remnants of our time past still cling to fence and cobweb still rustle in corridor and speak in hushed tones from overgrown garden beds – love is enough, I said, for this life – we who had nought but sacrifice, out of step with the moment the seasons – now I have nothing, you said, but at least now you know

the past dissolves its images bereft of sorrow, a barrow lays rusting in the rain and the raging howl of a woman betrayed by fate stirs uneasy a heart in need of rest – I note every murmur and sigh, shape images in order to understand the nightmare that inhabits the flesh – impossible to love beyond our differences, a bitter truth to learn, tainting all I'd hoped to gain the past I have to burn

there is grief still on the strangled road, the dark river flows yet, the stormy days of desire and will to be absolved – but justice lives in a dry canal, where roses never bloom, where Judas once fell down and wept that he'd ever been born

burial hot locust eve, the past, its bony finger now dust – beyond despising after all I'm only flesh and blood, drifting along tired cold streets – unique, confined, at times without fear reliving the tension my inheritance, the spade soil and sweat bound and tied to dreams not born of freedom, not knowing to whom I was trying to prove or why, nothing to spare

this lonely space, the cold consuming my flesh, the cried
river, the un-held hand, homeless waiting for death, because
love never stopped – the blade long fallen, now counting the
cost of wholeness, the value of life without you – the texts
that charted our trials our joy and perhaps our demise, well
the silverfish I've noticed and good riddance

turn about, if you can, if you dare, but I'm not your enemy
and I'm not your man, I'm not that dreamer now – I'm just
getting on with dying – another slow night torchlight
through trees, wilderness moon sleeping wren, all forgetting –
another year this room sings in the same dark remembering
you, yearning and turning away from life

last night I dreamed the fisted linesman, the hunched wife
shelling peas, but they wait no more their wayward son
smiles, turning at the window, another year undone – but
where to now by which route? still I suppose the heart, I've
tasted, had my fill of sadness now at the helm of a new day, I
wish to sing – one step to begin, toward the end waiting, in
full possession of mind and limb, no word of human
complaint, quietly on the heels of fate, the striking hour will
not come again.

twilight

the twilight of forgetting you
our life not forgotten
our love a tattered kite
hovers in the wind

I'm tired of this sadness
like falling rain on a long
and desolate street

I had a dream you were knocking
and in the darkness
I couldn't find the door.

resolve

two hours less to go, I feel dull, unprepared, she'll bring
a gift of course – the day warming and she will explain
something, which I may grasp to later forget –
I have money now, not a great deal and my father

gave me shirts and ties… I'll never wear them,
just another distraction, like the ozone,
like the trees we planted…
problems for the psyche, now a small forest…

this new game, dancing in the death throes,
the deck is stacked christ knows who dealt it,
reaching out from the chaos never knowing if
you thought it or felt it –
life devoid of family, ritual, solitude all the way,
to the gates of –
again at the beginning, one's devices – changing shape

today the cricket the heat, I wander down to visit old Alan
stiff one day lucid the next, we watch the test, in our silence
the comfort of acceptance, waiting for the cool of evening,
thinking, neglect is another kind of betrayal – loneliness
sucks you in but if the cup is empty, well – the cup, is empty.

cherry plum time

in a quiet mood slate wiped clean of past blood still stained at cross roads fingers beckon this way and that, I'm not blind call it indifference, generally stable expecting rain, I appreciate your understanding better late I suppose than never – Phoenix began whole shitload, came in waves thank god it didn't come all at once – bravado disintegrating living from habit rather than desire – needed compassion got derision, wanted joy got pain – thanks but I've had enough, now full of angst but no reason to give up in disgust, ride insidious wave come black whirlpool down to depths of – christ who needs it…days later totally wasted, but alive alive oh

for now enough as expected in a quiet mood – siblings can't face – too much pain in their eyes, trust in hate I don't play with love I won't when your soul's up for grabs lucky to escape with your shirt

– come children play with me – sing songs 'neath the Axle Tree what's up, Donny boy? maggot fear got yer tongue puppet strings an undone – 'ere lad…'ere's sixpence.

going home

the weather has started again, the sword turned inward
smouldering in the gutter the ashes of a life's work autumn –
autumn is the best time, don't you think? but Rachel I keep
losing my sense of humour the welled up brine so easily spills
– outside the three mounds where frost never sets, I think
yes, I've grieved enough

this holy game of being, no heroes, no answers, words strewn
across the table, an electric radiator keeps warm the big act –
at midnight Rick and I tramped through the pines we carried
sticks wrenches and a sledgehammer – to play the bridge, a
great concrete and steel span – we played with passion, trucks
roared through the eternity below, rhythms soared on the
wind – stumbling through it seems, this measured life,
loitering around closed doors, waiting, everything borrowed
from either yesterday or tomorrow – I write this world of
words with a blunt knife-pen, imagination is the bridge – you
can be anything what is it? a Sunday drive, another night in
front of the tube?

Friday evening lost and dismayed in the supermarket from
out of the blue, an old friend and Lydiard Street falls into
slow motion, smiling disbelief – but what do we know in the
hurried darkness, as we say good-bye?

the swallow

the swallow at the window hovers – noon dreams
recline on the couch, dipping into books, their word pools
shimmer and ripple, so much care like a well turned leg
as you pull on your stocking for an appointment

I hear your car drift down the lazy dusty road
I stir a slow hand examine the clear cold water and wonder
it sliding down my throat – should I surprise you with a meal
bake bread or perhaps get the gun, leave the sleeping noon
dream amble find a quiet glade, wait for a pair of ears
but I drift away deeper from prying thoughts, the sinking
comfort of the couch, the addictive lure of words

iron creaks, the sun climbs, somewhere in the distance
a pump kicks in, cockies screech and I'm woken with the news
book sprawled on the floor – dinner at Antonio's, I smile,
the thought of chess and port as I wander down to feed the hens.

weird uncle

it was another day, I felt like a tourist
hanging around with my empty cup
this foreign land, with so many people
doing crazy things for no apparent
reason – me included – but
life seemed friendly, within reach

I walked across the sand to the jetty
two fishermen and a boy sitting on the edge
feet dangling over, no bites, lines
shooting into the water at interesting angles
I caught the end of a conversation
this kid said to one of the men
you're a weird uncle.

www.ingramcontent.com/pod-product-compliance
Lightning Source LLC
Chambersburg PA
CBHW062142100526
44589CB00014B/1660